Shouts and Whispers

SHOUTS AND WHISPERS

Radical Meditations for Lent

By

Wake Forest University
School of Divinity Students and Guests

Edited by

Katherine A. Shaner

library partners press
a digital publishing imprint

ISBN 978-1618460523

Second printing

Copyright © 2018 by the Authors

Cover image: Dacian Woman, from the
Sebasteion in Aphrodisias, Turkey. Photo
used with permission of NYU-Aphrodisias
Excavations.

This work is licensed under a Creative
Commons Attribution-ShareAlike 4.0
International License

Produced and Distributed By:

Library Partners Press
ZSR Library
Wake Forest University
1834 Wake Forest Road
Winston-Salem, North Carolina 27106

a digital publishing imprint

www.librarypartnerspress.org
Manufactured in the United States of America

CONTENTS

INTRODUCTION

Return to the Lord, your God, who is gracious and
merciful, slow to anger and abounding in steadfast love.
Joel 2:13

Christians who observe Lent hear these words from
Joel every year as an invitation to spend the forty days
leading to Easter in holy reflection and intentional turning
toward God. This set of meditations invites you to this
holy and intentional work in just a few moments every day.

But this is not an ordinary or traditional Lenten
devotional. The daily meditations in this book were written
as part of a course entitled "Women and Slaves in the New
Testament" during the fall of 2017 at Wake Forest
University School of Divinity. The writers have wrestled
with some of the most difficult texts in the New Testament
and the broader Christian tradition—texts about enslaved
people, women, and the intersections of slavery and
misogyny.

When we first came together as a group of colleagues
from different racial, gender, class, and sexual identities,
from different faith traditions, with different politics,
pursuing theological education for different ends, none of
us was sure what to expect. We were all unsure whether or
with what parts of ourselves we could trust each other and
even God.

It is tempting to paint the story of this book as one in
which such a diverse group of people came happily to the

1

table, worked through the awkward tensions, the gut-wrenching emotions, the power dynamics, and the uncertainties of our collective endeavor, and formed a tight-knit family-like system that defies all the nastiness that our current moment in history has produced. But the truth is, we still wrestle with the ways that our own experiences as human beings—the very thing we should have in common—can divide us from each other.

This book is the hope-filled answer to fourteen weeks of working together. As a collective, each in our own way, we dove deeply into the pain, the guilt, the anger, anxiety, frustration, and despair at work in systems of slavery and misogyny. Our time together forced us to confront ways that slavery and assumptions of women's weakness are embedded in the Bible and our theologies. Amid that confrontation, we began to see, to experience, even to create a compulsion toward hope. The questions we thought were unaskable became the very place where hope, liberation, empowerment began to glimmer.

These daily meditations invite you into these questions—to examine the most basic ideas about our relationship to God. We often read Joel's words as a step-by-step process; grace, mercy, patience, abundance, unbreakable love are only ours once we abandon ourselves and return to the master. This set of meditations suggests a new formula for approaching Lent's days of introspection. The insights in this book begin from the conviction that our God *is already* gracious, merciful, patient, and abundantly, unbreakably loving.

In the certainty of that grace, mercy, patience, and steadfast love, we can then return to the hardest questions, the deepest doubts, and even the most socially taboo reflections about God.

We invite you to return to God, not in an attempt at being anyone other than who you are. Return to God with all your questions, all your wrestling, because you have never been and never will be outside of God's grace, mercy, patience, and steadfast love.

Katherine A. Shaner
Ash Wednesday 2018

ASH WEDNESDAY

Blandina was filled with such power, that those who tortured her one after the other in every way from morning till evening were wearied and tired. They admitted they were baffled. They had no other torture they could apply to her.
They were astonished that she remained alive.
Letter to the Churches of Vienne and Lyon, from Eusebius, *History of the Church* 5.1

Meditation

Blandina was a young slave girl in southern France who served a mistress who was a follower of Jesus. Blandina's mistress taught her about Jesus and the cross, but that wasn't enough for Blandina to be able to stand against the great and powerful authority of the Roman Empire in the second century CE. The Romans eventually seized Blandina, telling her she had no right to worship Jesus if the Empire told her to worship the gods of Rome. Blandina was called foolish. She was told that there was no way she could know more than the Emperor of Rome. Eventually, along with many other Christians, Blandina was sentenced to death, after which she would be remembered as one of the great Martyrs of Lyon. We can learn a lot about the roles of women—and specifically women who were slaves during the time of the Roman Empire—from the story of Blandina. Women's voices, especially enslaved women's voices, were silenced. They were silenced for having a voice of their own, but specifically for having a voice that spoke against the Roman Empire. We see this narrative time and time again. We watch as the voices of privilege continually silence the voices of the oppressed. We watch as the positions of power continually take the lives of those without power. We watch, and often we remain silent ourselves, not because we have been silenced, but because we choose to sit idly by and say nothing. May we learn from this enslaved woman of the Roman Empire that the voices of the oppressed must be heard, uplifted, and held, as these voices have tirelessly had to uplift themselves for far too long.

Invitation

As we journey through this season of Lent, may we ask ourselves whom we have silenced, and may we find our own voices to speak against those who are the silencers. Amen.

Emily Davis

DAY 2

To the unmarried and the widows I say that it is well for
them to remain unmarried as I am. But if they are not
practicing self-control, they should marry. For it is better
to marry than to be aflame with passion.

1 Corinthians 7:8–9

Meditation

As with each of the communities to which he wrote, Paul
wrote to the assembly in Corinth with answers to critical
questions of his day. Together, these communities and
Paul were struggling to figure out what morality looked like
as they sought to follow Jesus. In this selection from 1
Corinthians, Paul sought to address questions of sexual
immorality and marriage in the Corinthian community. As
with many of the answers found in Paul's letters, we find
the language problematic in our current environment. Not
only did Paul suggest that women may lack self-control and
thus be in need of a husband; he also argued that both
husband and wife lack control of their own bodies.

For our current faith communities, these ideas,
along with Paul's other takes on marriage and divorce
found in this passage, can cause harm. They have been
used to police women's bodies, to condemn the love of
same-sex couples, and to perpetuate sexist practices
around marriage. It is important to remember in examining
Paul's writings that, just as many in our communities today
do not agree with these arguments, communities in Paul's

day did not either. These conversations did not happen in a vacuum, but rather reflect arguments among communities that were trying to sort out how to follow Jesus. As with much of the biblical text, we must live in the tension, wrestling with destructive texts and finding solace in uplifting ones.

Invitation
Dearest God, help us to find courage in approaching all of our sacred texts, finding your gospel even when it seems obscured.

Marc DeCoste

DAY 3

Slaves, accept the authority of your masters with all deference, not only those who are kind and gentle but also those who are harsh. For it is a credit to you if, being aware of God, you endure pain while suffering unjustly.

1 Peter 2:18–19

Meditation

When I was a young girl my mentors taught me that obeying the Bible was the only way to secure salvation. When challenges came my way, I was supposed to be grateful and appreciative that God would entrust me with such hardships. The text in 1 Peter affirms this teaching, particularly in terms of addressing slavery. It is within this text that slaves are told to *endure*. This term typically means press on, disregard hardship, and ignore suffering—even if unjust. Although not widely discussed, slavery in ancient times was futile, horrific, and demeaning to say the least. Therefore, it is hard to see the connection between a God that came to set the captives free and a God that affirms the enslavement of their people. The lack of clarity from this text leads me back to the word "endure" and its function in the text itself. The text says, "you endure pain while suffering unjustly." The term "endure" ordinarily suggests a sense of self-preservation. However, in this text I believe it means something much different. I believe the word "endure" suggests a commitment to living a life where everything and everyone is made in the *imago dei*, image of God. This text is calling humanity to endure in the life-affirming truths of the Holy Spirit in light of a world that ignores and rejects anyone or anything that deviates from the norm. Together we can empower one another to endure the heart of the Lord by recognizing our own blind spots in our life. Community is the key to endurance, and we must remember we are not and never alone. To endure is not to accept hatred. To endure is to fight for the truth. To endure is to surround ourselves with the kin(g)dom of God. Endure my siblings, in the truth of the Lord. Endure.

Invitation

How do you need to re-author the term "endure" in your own life? How can this particular text remind us that no one owns us physically, emotionally, or mentally? How do we endure this truth event when it is hard?

Gretchen Joy Gabrielson

DAY 4

Mary took a pound of costly perfume made of pure nard,
anointed Jesus' feet, and wiped them with her hair. The
house was filled with the fragrance of the perfume.

John 12:3

Meditation

In this most holy moment of anointing, Jesus is prepared
for impending death—and what a preparation it is!
Imagine the magnitude of an aroma that can fill an entire
house. Consider a perfume that could cost a year's salary.
Ask yourself if you would wash the feet of another with
your own hair. Mary's actions serve as the model for how
we ought to sacrifice to God totally, willingly, and without
reservation. But, if we are not careful, this act of costly
devotion can be glamorized and commodified for 40 days
of selective service during the Lenten season.

This is why John is mindful to tell us that a woman—
an oppressed, marginalized, disenfranchised human—is
the vessel of ministry and blessing to the Messiah.

Her name is Mary, and she is someone who has already
had so much of her identity sacrificed and denied as
dictated by the systems around her.

Her name is Mary, and she is the embodiment of Black
and Brown women for whom denial and sacrifice is our
daily way of life. She is the cis, trans, queer, and woman
who willfully and without reservation pours herself out as
the winning votes in Alabama, the mothers of the

movements, the visitors in our prisons, and the caretakers of least of these.

Invitation
May we gather at the table in truth, admitting that we who have much do not sacrifice and only give some while those with less sacrifice and give all.

D'Najah Pendergrass

FIRST SUNDAY IN LENT

Jesus said also to the one who had invited him, "When you give a luncheon or a dinner, do not invite your friends or your brothers or your relatives or rich neighbors, in case they may invite you in return, and you would be repaid. But when you give a banquet, invite the poor, the crippled, the lame and the blind. And you will be blessed, because they cannot repay you, for you will be repaid at the resurrection of the righteous."

Luke 14:12–14

Meditation

In this passage Jesus shares banquette etiquette with fellow diners. After Jesus speaks the words above, another guest exclaims in verse 15, "Blessed is anyone who will eat bread in the kingdom of God!" Jesus tells of a time when someone held a banquet and invited a lot of people. The banquet's host sent his slave to gather the guests when the banquet was ready, but all of them gave excuses as to why they couldn't make it. This upset the host, so he sent his slave to invite people with physical disabilities and the poor until there was no more room because those invited would not be a part of his banquet. This parable is a direct response to the words spoken in verse 15. The eyes of that guest were set on the prize of the far-off kingdom of God, not on showing mercy to those less fortunate. We often hear, "Give so you can receive." But in this passage Jesus reminds us to give even when the favor cannot be returned.

It could be argued that anger and vindictiveness guided the host's actions. However, in the end, many people who were deemed 'undesirable' in the eyes of their society were treated to a great banquet. Many well-intentioned people do good, but often only so the favor will be paid back or so God will reward them in heaven. In the parable of the banquet, someone who perhaps did not start with the best intentions blessed those in need.

Invitation

Unlike the master of the banquet, God blesses God's children out of love. In this season of giving up let us also, with love, give to those in need.

Andrea Marulanda-Gutiérrez

DAY 5

On the contrary, the members of the body that seem to be weaker are indispensable, and those members of the body that we think less honorable we clothe with greater honor, and our less respectable members are treated with greater respect; whereas our more respectable members do not need this.

1 Corinthians 12:22–24

Meditation

Lent is a time of repentance and conversion. We examine our individual and collective conscience, we confess our sins, and we commit ourselves to re-turning to the path of faithful membership in Christ's Body. When Paul's first letter to the Corinthians tells us that we are many members of this one body, we often hear his message as a celebratory refrain of unity in diversity. In the spirit of Lenten repentance, though, I read this passage with a heavy heart and a lot of questions.

Paul offers a vision of human relationships here in which enslaved and free persons *both* have an integral role to play in the body, and neither one is dispensable. In fact, while the free person might imagine herself to be more important than the enslaved according to the world's standards, she is actually very much dependent on the enslaved and should therefore accord the enslaved person great honor and respect. Paul is right to draw our attention here to the dependence of privilege on the labor, suffering, and death of the disinherited. To give just one example, the privilege of inexpensive food on our tables usually depends on the near-enslavement of migrant farm workers. But how can we honor and respect the indispensable role of agricultural workers in the Body of Christ without acting to undo systems that bind them to unconscionable working conditions? Is it not mere lip service to celebrate unity in diversity, to honor enslaved and exploited workers as indispensable, without a commitment to undoing systems of enslavement and exploitation all together? In Christ's Body, the enslaved person is indispensable, but it is the salvific work of Christ's Body to dispense with enslavement.

Invitation

What forms of enslavement do you suffer and/or benefit from in your own life today? And how might the Body of Christ subvert these forms of enslavement?

Elizabeth O'Donnell Gandolfo

DAY 6

No one can serve two masters; for a slave will either hate
the one and love the other, or be devoted to the one and
despise the other. You cannot serve God and wealth.

Matthew 6:24

Meditation

When I'm at a party, I usually stick to the sides with a
beverage in hand in order to prevent awkward social
interactions. This is fine with me, but sometimes a
compassionate extravert will come up to me and engage in
conversation. This happened at a graduation party my
senior year of college.

Conversation was going pretty well, even though other
people were getting progressively louder. At one point, I
couldn't hear my new friend. "What?" I asked, at least three
times.

The last time, I understood what he said, but he still
punctuated, laughing, with, "Did I stutter?"

I laughed it off, but the conversation died soon after.
It's a common figure of speech, but as someone with a
severe stutter, I felt hurt by his comment.

This verse probably functioned similarly to that joke.
Some people would have understood it as most of us do,
as an illustration of the opposition between God's reign
and self-interest. Just as an enslaved person would favor
one master should she serve two, so too a disciple of Christ

must guard against greed and excessive focus on material prosperity.

But an enslaved person would probably have heard it differently. If no one can serve two masters, she might have felt excluded from a community in Christ since she already served a human master.

Even Jesus' words carried unintended, multiple meanings. What we say has the power to curse in spite of the best intentions—or to bless despite the worst.

Invitation

How might someone different from me hear my words? Can I be more careful? Can I give others grace for what they say?

Erica Saunders

DAY 7

Then the father said to him, "Son, you are always with
me, and all that is mine is yours. But we had to celebrate
and rejoice, because this brother of yours was dead and
has come to life; he was lost and has been found.

Luke 15:31–32

Meditation

We encounter a son in this story, often called the prodigal
son, who shows us what it means to be lost. He leaves his
home thinking that there is better out there, but soon
realizes the comfort and privilege that his father's money
gave him. Being lost for this son means thinking only of
himself and exploiting the kindness he is shown along the
way. While his father's slaves work hard for what they have,
he returns home as soon as he realizes the hard nature of
their work.

We often want to focus on the part when the son is
embraced and labeled "found," but the story doesn't
actually end there. We don't know if the rest of his family
and his father's slaves welcome the son back warmly. While
he rehearsed a good apology, we don't know if the prodigal
son truly repents of his destructive and privileged behavior.
We leave the prodigal son when he is still lost. Though he
has been embraced by his father, he has not yet been
found.

Believing that the son is no longer lost is a more
palatable ending because we often see ourselves in the

image of the prodigal son. But what if during this Lenten season we chose to name the ways in which we are lost? What if we admitted that we don't have it all figured out, that we have squandered what was given, that we have used our privilege to the detriment of others, and that we have hurt countless children of God in the process?

Maybe that is where God will find us and embrace us.

Invitation

God, help us to grow in the times where we feel lost. Lead us away from comfort and easy answers and dwell with us in the hard work of self-examination. Amen.

Sarah Parker

DAY 8

On the top of an ancient building in Aphrodisias in modern Turkey, where some of the largest Christian church buildings from antiquity are found, stands an image of the goddess Aphrodite. She sits in the nude, cross-legged, on top of a half-seashell, which is lifted out of the water. Two male tritons, or merpeople, flank each side of the shell, raising Aphrodite out of the sea, much like she raises each side of her wet hair above her shoulders.

Meditation

This image of Aphrodite is found on the Aphrodite Pediment within the Atrium House, located in Aphrodisias. Aphrodisias, an ancient Roman city located in modern-day Turkey, is named in honor of the Greek sea-goddess, Aphrodite. By uncovering these ancient artifacts that dust, dirt, and time have tried to hide within this city, we are given the rare opportunity to look back in time and imagine what spiritual worship of pagan gods and goddesses looked like in the ancient world. We quickly realize that being a "Christian" was not as clear-cut as we often idealize the earliest Christian communities to have been. But perhaps this difficulty reveals the truth that God does not work in a vacuum. Rather, God is constantly revealing God's self through the most peculiar and seemingly wonderful media. With this in mind, I wonder what God is revealing to us in this particular image of

Aphrodite. At first, it may seem rather off-putting to see a nude woman exalted to a divine status. After all, our Christian God has no consort and has traditionally been identified as male. Yet, as a Christian woman, I cannot help but feel empowered by this image of Aphrodite, a woman who is one with all aspects of herself, including her sexuality. Here she sits aloft the shell in confidence and self-love of her bodily temple, acknowledging its inherent goodness. Such an idea seems to contradict verses like Galatians 5:19, which speak openly about the deeds of flesh being immoral and impure. And yet, as always we find truth in Jesus, our Savior, who took flesh and *inhabited it*, experiencing its gifts and goodness, who revealed God's love and joy by touching, healing, and holding the broken bodies of God's people.

Invitation

Look around you. In what forms and media is God revealing truth to you? Have you embraced the joy and goodness that comes *from your flesh?*

Morgan Wehrkamp

DAY 9

But it is not so among you; but whoever wishes to
become great among you must be your servant, and
whoever wishes to be first among you
must be slave of all.

Mark 10:43–44

Meditation

Several of Jesus's disciples argue over who will be seated
next to him in glory, vying to become most powerful
among his early followers. Jesus, in response, calls for a
reorientation of the system, stating that in order to hold
power, one must not be above but rather under all. Using
the language of slavery, Jesus suggests that, among his
followers, the master is not the one with power, but rather
the enslaved person is. In this vein, Jesus "came not to be
served but to serve" (Mark 10:45). He shows us that we do
not become closer to God through limiting the voices of
others. Rather God calls us to serve others, putting
ourselves in vulnerable or risky positions for the
betterment of humanity. We are most powerful when we
abandon the power we have inherited in order to give to
those with less. During this Lenten season, we must ask
ourselves what power we may give up in the service of
others. Do we, as followers of Jesus, desire earthly
positions of power and authority and thus forget that our
ultimate power is in serving each other? Even within our
faith communities, we must be careful that our quests for

leadership or voice are not aimed at personal glorification, but rather at attending to the needs of our communities. In all that we do, we must never conflate our earthly roles with those that Jesus gave to us.

Invitation
Jesus, help us to love and serve one another, knowing that our reward is not in how much we accomplish or what we do, but rather in why we do it.

Marc DeCoste

DAY 10

For no one ever hates his own body, but he nourishes
and tenderly cares for it, just as Christ does for the
church, because we are members of his body.

Ephesians 5:29–30

Meditation

I had the good fortune of growing up with two fathers: my
biological father and, after his death, my stepfather. My
mom and dad made decisions jointly on important matters
and divided responsibilities for other parts of our lives.
They prayed together for guidance in decision-making and
nurturing their children. Mom and my stepfather followed
a similar pattern, praying together as they worked and
raised a family. Both marriages were loving and mutually
supportive, with each partner seeking God's best for their
lives together and operating out of their unique strengths.

Ephesians 5:22–33 provides a glimpse into family
relationships among Christians. The times were very
different—women possessed few rights, child protective
laws were unheard of, and slavery was actively practiced
among Christians and non-Christians alike. These
differences are no small matter. We must read these verses
in their own time and place. Then we can unearth the
jewels within.

When we look closely, we discover that the writer
proposes a way of being laced with love and mutual
accountability: "Be subject to one another out of reverence

for Christ" (Ephesians 5:21). Wives were to defer to their husbands, but the writer places a greater weight of responsibility upon the one with greater liberty and social standing, the husband. The husband's social and religious responsibility was to secure his wife's wellbeing, to practice love for her, esteem her highly, cherish her as he would his own body and as Christ does the Church.

Times have changed, and these ancient instructions were but a first step toward greater mutuality. Women and men lead in church and society, but Christian marriage remains a sacred bond laced with love and mutual accountability. Spouses still pray together, asking God to guide our decisions, strengthen our relationships, and protect our children.

Invitation

May we commit ourselves to practices of love and mutual respect, so that the love we have for ourselves and the love Christ has for the church might be reflected in the quality of our marital relationships.

Veronice Miles

SECOND SUNDAY IN LENT

There is no longer Jew or Greek, there is no longer slave
or free, there is no longer male and female; for all of you
are one in Christ Jesus.

Galatians 3:28

Meditation

As a trans woman, I hear echoes of Paul in attacks on my
womanhood today. Living into who I am, expressing my
femininity through clothing and makeup, adjusting my
body with medical interventions, "just perpetuates
misogynistic gender roles," I'm told. I should just do
what's expected of me as a person assigned male at birth,
since we're all the same on the inside anyway.

During Lent, we prepare ourselves for the death and
resurrection of Jesus and we suffer with him. Indeed, we
are reminded of this at the beginning of the season: we are
dust, and to dust we shall return (Genesis 3:19; Ecclesiastes
3:20). Yet Paul reminds us that just as we die with Jesus, so
too we rise with him (Romans 6:5). As Christians, we
embrace Lenten suffering in anticipation of the Easter
resurrection.

But maybe it isn't that simple. Could our good news
turn out to be fake news?

Our text sorts humanity into a series of simple
hierarchical categories: Jew over Greek, free over enslaved,
male over female. By denying these categories in favor of
unity in Christ, it encourages those on the bottom to

change. Free Jewish masculinity becomes the norm, a spiritual ideal. Enslaved Greek women are erased. The privileged remain privileged and the oppressed continue to be silenced.

But unity doesn't mean conformity. In Christ's resurrection, we transcend binaries instead of dismantling them. Perhaps joining Jesus on his journey means embracing our identities. Clothing ourselves with Christ (Galatians 3:27), we can acknowledge our similarity while celebrating our particularity.

Invitation

When I am tempted to reconcile differences, how can I affirm them instead?

Erica Saunders

DAY 11

Women should be silent in the churches. For they are not permitted to speak, but should be subordinate, as the law also says. If there is anything they desire to know, let them ask their husbands at home. For it is shameful for a woman to speak in church.

1 Corinthians 14:34–35

Meditation

Growing up in a progressive church, I always heard an easy explanation of our text in 1 Corinthians. Paul is writing to a certain congregation in a certain context, so we can't apply his words to our contexts today. At 15, this explanation proved good enough because it helped me rationalize my love of Paul's letters despite this problematic mandate to women.

Then I was called to ministry, and this explanation started to feel weak as men and women referred to my sermons as "talks" and used Paul's words against me to say I wasn't hearing God correctly.

Paul *is* speaking to a specific church in these verses. If we read the chapters leading up to 14, we see that the church is struggling with specific voices overpowering others and conflicts among those in the church. But Paul chooses an easy answer. Instead of looking at the ethic of Jesus, which teaches that even rejected Samaritan women can proclaim the Messiah's presence (John 4:1–29, see Third Sunday in Lent), Paul chooses to apply a Roman hierarchy that says women fall below men on the societal pyramid.

Truthfully, the Jesus ethic doesn't provide easy answers either. The Jesus ethic pushes us to examine our preconceived notions about people and societal norms, forcing us to make decisions that, quite often, place us in the minority. Like Paul, we often choose easy answers when there is discord in our communities. During this season of fasting, may we choose to fast from easy answers and comfortable solutions and seek the ethic of Jesus.

Invitation
God, give us the strength to challenge the status quo. Help us to question our communities' traditions and hierarchies that disenfranchise our siblings. Amen.

Sarah Parker

DAY 12

The owner of the house became angry and ordered his servant, "Go out quickly into the streets and alleys of the town and bring in the poor, the crippled, the blind and the lame." "Sir," the servant said, "what you ordered has been done, but there is still room." Then the master told his servant, "Go out to the roads and country lanes and compel them to come in, so that my house will be full. I tell you, not one of those who were invited will get a taste of my banquet."

Luke 14:21–24

Meditation

What we have here is a parable of Jesus that has often been used to teach us a story of ungratefulness (Luke 14:16–23). This main character of this tale feels betrayed and underappreciated when his friends make excuses towards his dinner party invitation. He really "shows them" by inviting those of a lower class into his home instead, saying that "not one of those who were *invited* will get a taste of my banquet."

There's an important detail we forget here. In this story, the less privileged, "the poor, the crippled, the blind, and the lame," are not considered the "invited" houseguests. Their presence is never preferred. It is used as a second choice, an act of spite towards these ungrateful friends who all have something better to do.

Who are the second round of dinner guests in our lives and in our world? Who are the people around us that we use and overlook?

I find myself guilty of doing this in my own life, as a white, middle-class woman. It is easy to give priority to those who look, think, and live like I do. It is easy to look up to people with the same amount of privilege. It is easy to see those with less money, power, and freedom as having less importance. But what would the world look like if we viewed the thoughts and feelings of persons who are homeless, impoverished, sick, abused, etc., with the same importance with which we viewed the most powerful and influential?

Invitation
God, give me the consciousness to be aware of those around me. Allow me to see the humanity in every person I encounter. May I see everyone as a welcomed guest at the table. Amen.

Jana Dye

DAY 13

"Then I saw an immense garden, and in it a gray-haired man sat in shepherd's garb; tall he was, and milking sheep. And standing around him were many thousands of people clad in white garments. He raised his head, looked at me, and said: 'I am glad you have come, my child.'"

The Martyrdom of Perpetua and Felicity

Meditation

As a hospital chaplain, I learned very quickly that there is nuance and shades of grey between past and future. I also learned that the image of the divine fluctuates between the stable, known divine figure and the God experienced in glimmers of tragedy and hope when stability seems impossible.

Today's selection from *The Martyrdom of Perpetua and Felicity* strikes me as this kind of experience. Perpetua is a woman from the second century who has been sentenced to death in a public spectacle in North Africa. She tells the story of a vision where she climbs a ladder, and this passage is a description of what she sees when she reaches the top. There is enough that is recognizable here to identify the references: the Garden of Eden, the thousands of saints dressed in white (Revelation 4), even the gray-haired God figure.

Immediately after this scene we see Perpetua meet her father before her execution. He is described as having "gray hair" as well. Might we consider what Perpetua felt putting those two realities together? There is a vision of a welcoming God who calls Perpetua "my child" and an earthly father who does not understand her. There is a vision for a future hoped for and the experience of a past that does not comprehend its impact. There is the God who invites and welcomes to something new and a world that holds tightly and begs to bring things back to the way they were.

Invitation
Write two lists of attributes of God. One list should be the attributes people "tell you God is" and the other a list of "who you experience God as." How might you share your unique experience of God with those around you, either through words or actions?

G. Travis Woodfield

DAY 14

But any woman who prays or prophesies with her head unveiled disgraces her head—it is one and the same thing as having her head shaved. For if a woman will not veil herself, then she should cut off her hair; but if it is disgraceful for a woman to have her hair cut off or to be shaved, she should wear a veil.

1 Corinthians 11:5–6

Meditation

Across many religious practices, the requirement for head coverings for women were often centered around the theme of modesty. The question we must ponder and ask: Why is the imposition of modesty only related to women? Women were created with the power of choice. Thus, head coverings should be approached as a sacred spiritual practice that derives from choice rather than requirement. Head coverings should not be a cloak of shame. What exactly is a woman required to hide? Historically, we have witnessed women be required to cover themselves. Women have been marked with scorn, with a reprieve that communicates messages of shame that lurks in the shadows of their divine power.

That which is made for shame should be a choice of liberation.

It is time for women to hold truth to who they divinely are.

It was the power of the Divine that empowered Jesus to walk in this earth. It was the power of the Divine that gave Jesus authority over that which attempted to subjugate and at times shame him. Embrace your divine power! Unleash it in this earth for all to behold and see!

Invitation

How can we change our communities so that practices which oppress or shame women might be regarded as a sacred choice, something that women choose for themselves?

Mia Hash Sloan

DAY 15

Then the LORD God said, "It is not good that the man
should be alone; I will make him a helper as his partner."
… Then the man said, "This at last is bone of my
bones and flesh of my flesh; this one shall be called
Woman, for out of Man this one was taken."

Genesis 2:18, 23

Meditation

Helper or slave? Equal or subordinate? These are just some
of the questions that can be generated when examining
Genesis 2:18, 23. Globally, women face many issues
ranging from lack of access to education to lacking the
right to make choices about their reproductive health. Here
in the United States, specifically, women have been under
attack. You can turn on the television, check your timeline
or tweets, and see cases of sexual assault on a daily basis.
You can walk into a major Fortune 500 company and find
a woman that is paid less than her male counterpart doing
the same job. Is this what God intended the fate of women
to be at that moment in the garden in Genesis 2?

Some would say yes. Women, through this traditional
lens, were created to be wife, lover, mother, exclusively
paired with a single man. Unfortunately, many of the
scenarios of injustice that women face globally, including
those above, are created by the conditions under which we
historically interpret the text to reflect our society. If we re-
examine this narrative, the creation of the woman brings

balance. The man was lonely in this garden, and God said that it was not good for man to be alone. The woman is a symbol of equity and not inequity. The woman comes into creation with her autonomy and not just a sense of being an empty vessel under the rule of man. Her very essence brings hope, a hope that life will flourish. In her a world of possibilities is birthed.

Invitation
How can we begin to value and uphold the equity of women?

Latricia Giles

DAY 16

The woman was clothed in purple and scarlet, and
adorned with gold and jewels and pearls, holding in her
hand a golden cup full of abominations and the impurities
of her fornication; and on her forehead was written a
name, a mystery: "Babylon the great, mother of whores
and of earth's abominations." And I saw that the woman
was drunk with the blood of the saints and the blood of
the witnesses to Jesus. When I saw her, I was greatly
amazed. But the angel said to me, "Why are you so
amazed?"

Revelation 17:4–7a

Meditation

I remember the first time a male wouldn't shake my hand
like it was yesterday. Why wasn't he willing to touch hands?
Simply because I am a woman? The frustration I felt was
paralyzing. How could I be deemed unworthy of a modest
greeting? Upon consideration of this experience I realized
that this gentleman was scared. He was scared of my body.
He was scared of losing power. He was scared that I would
somehow take something valuable away from him. This
experience mirrors the depiction of the rejected woman in
Revelation 17. I find great comfort in the woman described
in this particular text. The woman was not only feared, but
judged, manipulated, and interpreted as other. Isn't this the
same way that the gentleman who wouldn't shake my hand
saw me? Judgments are immediately made about women

more often than by women. This new way of thinking allows us to reconsider the way that women are depicted throughout history and especially within this image in Revelation 17. I find solace that I am not the only woman, nor the first woman, who has received this sort of reaction from a man. This woman, sometimes called the Whore of Babylon, isn't someone or something to be ashamed of. Instead, she provides comfort for those who find themselves outside of what society deems as valuable. This woman invites us to see the *imago dei*, the image of God, within all of us, and for that I am grateful.

Invitation

The *imago dei* is within you and within all of us. Remind yourself of this when you feel unworthy or insignificant in the face of others' judgments.

Gretchen Joy Gabrielson

THIRD SUNDAY IN LENT

The woman said to him, "Sir, I see that you are a prophet. Our ancestors worshiped on this mountain, but you say that the place where people must worship is in Jerusalem." Jesus said to her, "Woman, believe me, the hour is coming when you will worship the Father neither on this mountain nor in Jerusalem... The woman said to him, "I know that Messiah is coming" (who is called Christ). "When he comes, he will proclaim all things to us." Jesus said to her, "I am he, the one who is speaking to you."

John 4:19–26

Meditation

Many readings of this encounter detail the way that Jesus serves as the mechanism for the Samaritan woman to overcome the sinfulness of her various marriages and sexual relationships. Her redemption comes by way of her going to the people of Samaria to tell them about Jesus and subsequently bringing them to meet him. This interpretation, however, leaves no room for the reality of her situation as a woman in ancient Samaria—living in a social and economic system that requires her to have connection to a male in order to be cared for and respected. It also leaves no room for her to have depth of character; this text presents her as intelligent and aware of who Jesus may be. We do not give her credit for these qualities. The woman engages in a debate with Jesus, acknowledging his wisdom and insight into her life experience by calling him a prophet. She continues to engage him by entering a sophisticated debate about the religious traditions of their people. For this period of Lent, I propose that Christians take a look at who we think Jesus is and interrogate it based on the model that the Samaritan woman displays for us in order that we might find a deeper truth. I would encourage us to look beyond the account of her life by condensing it down to her sexual or marital history. Instead, we should read this text as it displays an intelligent Samaritan woman who has the ability to interrogate her own tradition.

Invitation

May we see the Samaritan woman as a model for how to interrogate our understandings of who Jesus is for us while recognizing the humanity in her and women like her.

Taina Diaz-Reyes

DAY 17

Let each of you remain in the condition in which you
were called. Were you a slave when called? Do not be
concerned about it. Even if you can gain your freedom,
make use of your present condition now more than ever.
For whoever was called in the Lord as a slave is a freed
person belonging to the Lord, just as whoever was free
when called is a slave of Christ. You were bought with a
price; do not become slaves of human masters.

1 Corinthians 7:20–23

Meditation

Today's text can, for good reason, leave us with some
mixed emotions. The frank discussion of slaves and
masters as a parallel for people and God—a parallel that
indicates the slave culture in the Roman Empire—can
leave us with a bad taste in our mouths (as it should). This
is the issue that comes with reading a text written in a
different time and culture, one that found acceptable things
we would shutter at today.

The hard truth is that we, modern people of faith, also
live in an unethical society. We may not personally own or
know anyone who owns slaves, but we constantly
participate in a system that advocates slavery and the abuse
of other human beings. It may not be our intention to do
this but, sadly, that is how our economic system is set up.
The things we buy and sell are usually produced,
somewhere in their production cycle, via slave labor.

It would be close to impossible for us to completely rid ourselves of these products; we enjoy and depend upon inexpensive clothing, for example. But in this season of moderation and reflection, what are ways that we can abstain from buying things made in unethical conditions? The text tells us to "make use of your present condition now more than ever." What are ways that we can make the best out of our current positions in life——a condition makes us unwilling participants in an economy that uses and abuses human beings? What are small acts of resistance we can accomplish in order to say we don't support this part of our society?

Invitation
How can we use out "present condition" for good? What if, each day of Lent, we challenged ourselves to replace one unethically produced item with an ethically produced one?

Jana Dye

DAY 18

Likewise, tell the older women to be reverent in behavior, not to be slanderers or slaves to drink; they are to teach what is good, so that they may encourage the young women to love their husbands, to love their children, to be self-controlled, chaste, good managers of the household, kind, being submissive to their husbands, so that the word of God may not be discredited.

Titus 2:3–5

Meditation

In *Practical Magic* (1998), Sandra Bullock and Nicole Kidman are grown sisters in the house of their aunts, Stockard Channing and Dianne Wiest; they happen to be witches. As it normally goes in such stories, the younger characters try to keep a crisis from their aunties, wishing to avoid the older women's eccentricities. The younger women want to appear normal in the eyes of the world.

Nothing escapes the aunties, however.

When all is quiet in the house, they initiate a margarita party in the middle of the night. A wildly ethereal scene ensues—women talking, dancing, cackling, and being deeply present in flesh and bone and spirit. The women look into one another and are seen as they are. Through the forming of their circle, the crisis is brought to the fore and the aunties create room for the younger women to learn and respond in the fullness of their innate ingenuity.

The women refuse to allow a crisis to isolate them from one another, and the story flows on from there.

From an outsider's perspective, the raucous dancing, irreverent laughter, and lavish libations of this midnight women's circle could seem eerily improper. Their actions could be interpreted as immoral or irresponsible. But that would not be fair. This cross-generational gathering was communion, reconciliation, and orientation for the good.

I wonder if the author of Titus 2 was like an outsider peering into the women's circle of his community, seeking erroneously to censor that which he did not understand.

Invitation

How might the women addressed in Titus lead us to expand our perceptions of propriety and lean into the liberation of Christ?

Leanna Coyle-Carr

DAY 19

Jesus replied, "It is not right to take the children's bread and toss it to the dogs." "Yes it is, Lord," she said. "Even the dogs eat the crumbs that fall from their master's table."

Matthew 15:26–27

Meditation

Such harsh words from our beloved Jesus! In Matthew 15: 21–28 a Syrophoenician woman, referred to as a Canaanite, approached Jesus and asked him to show compassion to her daughter, who was possessed with a demon. Jesus ignored her, and the disciples asked him to make her go away because her cries were bothering them. Jesus states that he was sent to help Israelites in need, but the woman kneels before him and asks him once more to help her. Then we have their difficult exchange in verses 26 and 27. Jesus is amazed with her faith and grants her request. Although it is shocking to hear Jesus call the Syrophoenician woman a dog, it was a common derogatory term for outsiders at the time.

How could Jesus use such derogatory language toward someone so vulnerable? How could Jesus deny a miracle to someone in need? Perhaps Jesus was shocked that a Gentile would have such faith in him when most Israelites didn't. Perhaps he wanted to test her, see how far she would go to get her miracle. She, a vulnerable Canaanite mother, spoke "out of order" to an Israelite man. Most importantly, she argued with the Son of God because she knew he had the power to heal her daughter. If Jesus listened to her argument, how much more should we listen to the people in our community begging for crumbs to survive while we feast?

Invitation

This season of Lent, let us extend our mercy to those we consider "the other." Let us be in communion with them and allow them to teach us and surprise us.

Andrea Marulanda-Gutiérrez

DAY 20

Suddenly Jesus met them and said, "Greetings!" And they came to him, took hold of his feet, and worshiped him. Then Jesus said to them, "Do not be afraid; go and tell my brothers to go to Galilee; there they will see me."

Matthew 28:9–10

Meditation

I grew up hearing, "Women should not preach," and I could never understand the difference between a woman preacher and man preacher. Living in a world where women have been oppressed by the church, I find this pericope to be hopeful for women. In this text, Jesus is speaking to Mary after his resurrection. The disciples—all men—have left the scene, but Mary stayed. Jesus speaks to her and tells her to go to tell the brothers that he is risen. We are supposed to preach the gospel of Jesus, which is the good news that Christ is risen from the dead. Since this is true, Mary is actually the first preacher of the Gospel. Jesus believed in women preachers because he sent the first woman preacher out. In this text, we can find hope that women in ministry may find their liberation from the oppression of this misogynistic world. Also, it is the hope that men in ministry may understand and accept that our Lord and Savior Jesus Christ believed and established women in ministry. Through this season may we reflect on this work of Christ: after his resurrection, he sent forth a woman as the first preacher into the world. Through this season may we find hope and liberation that God has ordained and selected women to serve in various capacities in ministry. May they share with men, women, boys, and girls the good news of Jesus Christ, risen from the dead!

Invitation

Let us pray: LORD, may women find liberation to work in ministry settings without the oppression and traditions of the church. May the church look to Jesus as an example of women having equal rights in ministry. Amen.

James H. Wilkes Jr.

DAY 21

Peter said [to Mary], "Tell us the words of the Savior which
you remember, which you know, but we do not, nor have we
heard them." Mary answered and said, "What is hidden from
you I will proclaim to you."

Gospel of Mary 5:6–7

Meditation

The *Gospel of Mary* is a post-resurrection account written in the
voice of Mary Magdalene. The disciples circle around Mary,
asking her to share with them the knowledge Jesus has given her.
Mary is shown as an authority figure with knowledge and access
to Jesus. This access is something that the disciples, such as
Peter, look to gain from her. And Mary agrees to *proclaim* from
her knowledge.

Mary becomes a part of the continuation of the good news
of Jesus Christ. In this gospel Mary is powerful, wise, and
proclaiming. As in the biblical gospels, Mary desires to seek the
wisdom of the Christ. She listens to Jesus's parables, she shares
meals with him, and witnesses his death and resurrection.

Yet Mary Magdalene's reputation has been tarnished.
Perhaps because she was a powerful, wise, and proclaiming
woman among a group of male disciples, her sexuality has been
exploited in order to discredit her. The evolution of Mary's
reputation mirrors that of women in religious leadership today.

Women are pushed to the side. Women are not allowed to
share what Christ has taught them. Women have their character
challenged when they share stories of pain and joy. But women
have wisdom to share.

In this passage from Mary's Gospel, Peter asks Mary for her
wisdom because she had something he does not. With the

shutting out of so many voices, what has the church refused to hear because of gender, sexuality, race, or class? What is the church missing today?

Invitation

Lent is a time of fasting, repentance, and listening to Christ. I invite you to be like Peter and to listen to what the Lord has to offer through the voices of those pushed to the margins. Allow the women in your life to be heard.

Mary's power in this story lies in her willingness to share her wisdom with the crowd. I also invite you to be the Mary within your community and to allow yourself to feel worthy of sharing what Christ has shared with you.

Angel Woodrum

DAY 22

Then I saw a new heaven and a new earth; for the first
heaven and the first earth had passed away, and the sea
was no more. And I saw the holy city, the new Jerusalem,
coming down out of heaven from God, prepared as a
bride adorned for her husband.

Revelation 21:1–2

Meditation

Revelation 21 presents an apocalyptic vision of what will
be when our current world is no more. In this vision, we
see a new a place in which God dwells among humankind,
where suffering and sadness is no more (Revelation 21:3–
4). We can imagine, in this revelation, a place where the
pain of those marginalized in our current society will be
eliminated as God's love replaces lament and mourning.
However, this text also has other implications for followers
of Christ. It is a call to our present world just as much as it
represents hope for what is yet to come. While Revelation
21 is an apocalyptic text, painting a picture of something
yet to come, it also differs from other literature of its kind.
It calls for our new world to be exactly where we stand
today.

God's dwelling, in this passage, is not in some distant
cosmic reality, but rather among humanity. This text is a
charge to improve the lives among us today. It is a call to
action, one that prevents us from avoiding the suffering
around us and pushes us out of a place of passivity. If

God's kingdom is closer than we think, we need to be concerned about what world we create. In these days of Lent, let us examine what we may do, to bring the kingdom of heaven closer in our present reality.

Invitation
God, you called us into communion with yourself and each other. Help us to bring your kingdom closer, a place where crying and pain are no more.

Marc DeCoste

FOURTH SUNDAY IN LENT

Look and see the place which is opened for you; there your eternal abode shall be, and there you will receive the beatific vision.

Acts of Paul and Thecla 11.6

Meditation

Where do we find our beatific vision? What *is* beatific vision? The word beatific means happy, blessed, heavenly, divine. Many who study theology understand it to be the ultimate, direct self-communication of God to the individual person, and theologians like Thomas Aquinas believe that this is something that you can only achieve in death. In the *Acts of Paul and Thecla*, we have this woman, a woman who, at first glance, you might say is crazy or perhaps merely infatuated with the apostle Paul. The reality is Thecla is a woman who marches to the beat of her own drum. After she hears Paul's preaching on chastity and celibacy, she is compelled to give up the life she knew to become a Christian and spread the gospel.

Thecla's rebellion and act of creating agency for herself made her a traitor to her community, a community that found it customary for women of a certain caliber to be married and have babies. She resisted the socio-cultural norms and the uncertainty that came with it, up to the point of death. It is not always an easy—heck, it is not always the most logical—decision to follow the voice of the divine. Many times, it can cost us friends and family, money, or even our lives. So, I will ask again: where do we find our beatific vision? If you're like Thecla, you resist the norms and become an example for women across generations.

Invitation
Be bold, be courageous, stand up for righteousness, and stand strong for justice. In your quest to find your beatific vison, continue to listen to the Divine.

Latricia Giles

DAY 23

Keep awake, therefore, for you know
neither the day nor the hour.
Matthew 25:13

Meditation

I've never been to a wedding like the one Matthew describes. The wedding party waits around until midnight, when the groom arrives, and then the party finally starts. But then a few flashlight batteries die, and half the bridesmaids are banished from the reception because they can't find any more. At midnight.

As is often the case, the absurd language of Matthew 25:1–13 is a clue to us that Jesus is talking about something other than what appears on the surface. The story may have originally been used to discredit women's voices, but the final draft is set in a much larger block of Jesus' storytelling. These stories are focused on how Jesus's followers should behave until he comes back, which would mean that this wedding is really about that return.

And, radically, women are present when Jesus comes back. The world these women inhabited rabidly favored men. The very story in which they appear may have originally been used to harm them. But in Jesus's kingdom, they are welcomed as equals.

That's what the oil is about, by the way. Whenever Jesus speaks about the end, there are some people who are prepared (i.e., they have been doing the good works of

Jesus) and some are not. While we want the oil to be shared, it's a symbol of the kind of inner work that cannot truly be shared. Women are welcomed as equals in the kingdom, with the same responsibility to be prepared for Jesus's return.

Invitation
Today, meditate upon this vision of Jesus' kingdom, one where the unjust norms of society are ignored and women get in, too.

Aaron Coyle-Carr

DAY 24

There is no longer Jew or Greek, there is no longer slave
or free, there is no longer male and female; for all of you
are one in Christ Jesus. And if you belong to Christ,
then you are Abraham's offspring,
heirs according to the promise.

Galatians 3:28–29

Meditation

The concept of being an heir, inheriting the promises of
God given to the Jews that are now available through faith
in Jesus, is repeated throughout the second and third
chapters of Galatians. Galatians 3:28–29 is the
acknowledgement of the work God has done to ensure
that all who "are one in Christ Jesus" have become
"Abraham's offspring" and therefore eligible for inclusion
into the covenant of inheritance as Abraham's
descendants. But later in chapter 4 (Galatians 4:21–5:1), the
text mentions Hagar and her son, Ishmael. They were both
expelled from Abraham's house after being told that
neither would receive any inheritance from their house—
despite Ishmael being Abraham's actual first-born son.
Slaves had no rights to inheritance, which Paul resists in
the larger argument of Galatians: the inheritance of slaves
who believe in Christ does not come in the form of wealth
or property. For the enslaved, Galatians' readers can the
claim that faith in Christ and an absorption into the
promise of God removes the worldly consequences of

enslavement. Although we note the harsh reality of slavery in the ancient world, Paul is conveying that Jesus's ministry, death, and resurrection bind anyone who believes, who would otherwise have no claim to a nation—including the enslaved—to hold membership among God's people. More importantly, beginning with Hagar, God includes those who have no worth, honor, or inheritance in the oppressive social and economic system of slavery into the promise of life and inheritance that comes through Jesus.

Invitation

God, give us wisdom to see and share the inheritance of full communion and restoration that you promise to all, despite the social limitations we place on others.

Taina Diaz-Reyes

DAY 25

For a bishop, as God's steward, must be blameless; he must not be arrogant or quick-tempered or addicted to wine or violent or greedy for gain; but he must be hospitable, a lover of goodness, prudent, upright, devout, and self-controlled.

Titus 1:7–8

Meditation

How would the world be different if young women held authority roles? Naturally, the world's history of favoring men deems women ill-equipped for the responsibilities of leadership. In Paul's letter to Titus, he explains that appointed figures in the church should be men who are not corrupt in any way. His version of an ideal leader is an example of the perfect man. Paul echoes still in today's society—a society that continues to hold that women are unfit to be in roles of authority. Then and now, there are men who do not serve those that they lead. Including silenced female voices would lessen the world's brokenness.

The assumption of authority as power continues to pervade society. Barbara Streisand once commented that women are understood as "demanding" while men are seen to be "commanding." During Jesus' life, his disciples called him "teacher," not "leader." In a world that values power and control, instead of leading by command or demand, our authority figures should be teaching and empowering. As a society, we need to teach our children that it's okay for men and women both to be in positions of authority. We should especially encourage young girls, even though there might not be many women to look up to as role models. They can be their own role models. Teach them how to use their voices so that their voices will be heard. Then teach them how to follow through on that promise and hear them.

Invitation
Write a letter in your voice to a young boy describing the value of women's voices and ways they can empower young women to let their voice be heard.

Aubrey Naugle

DAY 26

"I believed it necessary to procure the truth from two slave women, whom they called deacons, by means of torture. I found nothing but a perverse, unreasonable religion carried out to extravagant lengths."
Pliny the Younger, *Letters to Trajan* 10.96.8[1]

Meditation

As a single minister, it can be hard to find a romantic partner. Church isn't quite like a bar or club, and you can't really flirt during the passing of the peace. So, like many other women my age, I have a few dating apps on my smartphone. You can more or less control your image on dating apps. You choose the photos you display and the bio you share. On Tinder, I don't have to be pigeonholed as The Preacher.

But I do get pigeonholed as a trans woman. People— usually cisgender, heterosexual men—always ask about what it means to be transgender or what's in my pants. Rarely do they conceive of me as a whole, complex person with interests, hobbies, and dreams.

In our text Pliny the Younger reduces the Christian deacons to their status as enslaved women. As a Roman governor, he tried to quell the spread of the Jesus movement. Earlier in his letter to the emperor Trajan, he mentions interviews with other Christians, but he only

---

[1] Translated from the Latin by Erica Saunders.

tortures the enslaved women. He knew that Roman courts would only accept testimony of enslaved persons if given under torture. Thus, Pliny viewed the deacons primarily as enslaved women, not as community leaders or even Christians. How much more would we know about early Christian communities had Pliny taken them more seriously, recording more detail? Pliny saw these women as Tinder profiles. What if he (and my Tinder matches) could see more than that?

Invitation

Seek out "sonder," or the realization that each random passerby is living a life as vivid and complex as your own, in a conversation today.

Erica Saunders

DAY 27

He looked all around to see who had done it. But the
woman, knowing what had happened to her, came in fear
and trembling, fell down before him, and told him the
whole truth. He said to her, "Daughter, your faith has
made you well; go in peace, and be healed of your
disease." *Mark 5:32–34*

Meditation

In college, a male classmate said to me, "Emily, you know
that you can't go on to be a minister, right?" This classmate
and I had been through this time and time again, and each
time I left with a sense of fear. What if I shouldn't pursue
this calling that I knew I needed to follow? I felt valid in
these feelings, even if I knew that they were just simply
feelings of fear.

In Mark's gospel, we encounter a woman who is sick
and ailing with each passing day. This woman thought that
if she could only touch Jesus's clothes that she'd be made
well. However, this wasn't an easy task, as the woman
would have to fight through many obstacles. Nevertheless,
she accomplishes this task and immediately feels healing.
Yet after hearing Jesus acknowledge that someone has
touched him, she feels guilt and shame. Jesus tells this
woman that "her faith has made her well and that she
should leave in peace." But isn't Jesus's saying yet another
example of a woman being told how she should feel or
what she should do? Maybe those fearful thoughts I

experienced in college crept in her mind. "What if I shouldn't have pursued this calling to be healed?" This woman, valid in her feelings, must be given the agency to feel as she will, think as she will, and do as she will, even when that means going against what has once brought healing and a sense of purpose.

Invitation
If you find yourself identifying as the woman, ask yourself where in your life you are feeling fear for what is necessary. If you find yourself identifying as Jesus, ask yourself how you are using your privilege to police the agency of people with less privilege.

Emily Davis

DAY 28

But the aim of such instruction is love that comes from a
pure heart, a good conscience, and sincere faith. Some
people have deviated from these and turned to
meaningless talk, desiring to be teachers of the law,
without understanding either what they are saying or the
things about which they make assertions.

1 Timothy 1:5–7

Meditation

First Timothy is set up as a sort of outline originally meant
for the church of Ephesus, but it has been used often by
modern churches as a blueprint for setting up the structure
of their institutions. Many of the instructions found in 1
Timothy have been used over the centuries to create
problematic congregational policies such as limiting
women's roles in ministry. Our verses for today can serve
as a helpful reminder of how to be effective faith leaders
in and outside of the church.

The author of 1 Timothy in this passage places an
emphasis on church leaders displaying authenticity,
morality, and sincerity. They are quick to point out that not
all ministers have possessed these traits. The author speaks
of people "desiring to be teachers of the law," but not
committing *themselves* to the law or taking time to really
understand the very concepts they preach and teach. These
people, the verses would claim, are wasting time with
"meaningless talk."

This passage can be used as a relevant instruction for modern people of faith. Far too often, we see Christians and Christian leaders who are much quicker to speak than they are to learn or listen. How many people have you seen, repeated, or posted Bible verses as an argument without understanding the cultural or historical context that they came from? How many ministries have you heard of or taken part in whose policies and structure contradict the Christ that they claim to represent? This passage reminds us of the dangers of false teaching.

Invitation
God, may we know what it means to be *authentic* teachers of the faith. May our teaching be motivated by love and not by our own self-fulfillment. Amen.

Jana Dye

FIFTH SUNDAY IN LENT

Surely, from now on all generations will call me blessed.

Luke 1:48b

Meditation

Finding your voice is hard. It is even harder when an author buries that voice behind the name of God. Today's reading from the Gospel of Luke (Luke 1:46–55) is one of the three "songs" attributed to Luke. The other two, the song of Zachariah (Luke 1:68–79) and the song of Simeon (Luke 2:29–32), speak of God's power and work in history. The text today, Mary's song, is a testament to the frustrating parts of finding God's engagement in the world.

Mary, the mother of Jesus, goes to visit her relative, Elizabeth, who is the mother of John the Baptist. Both Jesus and John have not been born yet. When Mary sees Elizabeth, John jumps for joy in her womb. Mary sings this song, sometimes called the Magnificat, in response.

The story is framed as two women—two pregnant women—meeting and the result of that meeting is the glorification of God. However, it is problematic that Mary's song has very little to do with Mary—or Elizabeth for that matter. The song deals with God's work in the world through time, and these women are vehicles to continue that story. Their stories, the stories of the women present in the scene, are forgotten to the broader place in the historical narrative.

Lent calls us into a time of reflection not only of how we fit into the story of the world, but also how we participate in that narrative. The "songs" we sing will be what "make us blessed" for generations to come.

Invitation

Think of the narratives that define you, for good or for ill, whether religious, cultural, political, social, or otherwise. Write a "song" that describes how you want to remembered and ways you can make that song reality.

G. Travis Woodfield

DAY 29

Peter answered and spoke concerning these same things.
He questioned them about the Savior, "Did he really
speak privately with a woman and not openly to us? Are
we to turn about and all listen to her?
Gospel of Mary 9:3–4

Meditation

In the *Gospel of Mary*, Mary Magdalene presents her vision of Christ to the other disciples. Mary is proclaiming a teaching Christ shared with her, and when she finishes sharing she is doubted. First, she is doubted by Andrew and then by Peter (Gospel of Mary 9:2-4). Then, Mary weeps (Gospel of Mary 9:5).

Five years ago, I was in a course called "Women and Philosophy" at Georgetown College. After a particularly heavy discussion on Aristotle's beliefs that women are intellectually, biologically, and authoritatively inferior, I went to the bathroom in our student center and cried. During the class I felt frustrated and enraged because I realized for the first time that the world today is not much different for women.

We are doubted when we share our ideas.

We are doubted when we share our feelings.

We are doubted when we share our stories.

We are Mary Magdalene.

But the good news of the *Gospel of Mary* is that, despite Peter's doubts about the relationship Mary shared with

Jesus, our biblical gospels show us that Mary is not to be doubted. Jesus and Mary did have a friendship. Their friendship was so strong that Mary was with Jesus when he drew his last breath (Matthew 27:56; Mark 15:40; Luke 23:49; John 19:25). Mary was the first to see him at the empty tomb (Matthew 28:1–8; Mark 16:9–10; Luke 24:10; John 20:18). Mary was a disciple, and that fact we should never doubt.

Invitation

During the Lenten season of repentance, consider those people and stories you have doubted. Give yourself a moment to wonder why you doubt. Challenge yourself to listen to those around you as Christ would listen to them.

Angel Woodrum

DAY 30

A great portent appeared in heaven: a woman clothed
with the sun, with the moon under her feet, and on her
head a crown of twelve stars. She was pregnant and was
crying out in birth pangs, in the agony of giving birth.

Revelation 12:1–2

Meditation

Giving birth is one of those experiences where women
exhibit the divine power to bring forth life, much like God
who brought forth life to every created thing. Although
this act of childbearing is in its end result often filled with
joy and happiness, we forget the birth process comes with
pangs and pains that a woman must endure *before* she is able
to give life. Here the woman clothed with the sun stands
on the moon and is nearing the end of her pregnancy. Yet
it is not only birth pangs that threaten her unborn child,
but also a great red dragon who creeps patiently near the
woman.

This dragon is waiting for the child to be delivered so
that he might swipe it up at her feet and devour this infant
who is prophesied to rule all the nations. When the child is
born, a son, God quickly intervenes, taking the son to the
heavenly throne while also preparing a place in the
wilderness for the mother to be nourished and safe. If we
wanted to, we could stop here in the story—reading this
narrative with a simple and happy ending. Yet I can't help
but question what it would feel like for this new mother to

have endured the long months of pregnancy only to have her child taken from her, even if he was taken by God.

Invitation
When Jesus was crucified, Mary wept for her son—she grieved his loss even while she knew he would be safe with God. We, too, are allowed to feel loss and to recognize that not all of life's experiences make sense, especially when we try to comprehend God's action or inaction in the midst of our suffering.

Morgan Wehrkamp

DAY 31

I am sending him, that is, my own heart, back to you.
Philemon 10

Meditation

Is it possible to be righteous in a world full of structural societal injustice and sin? Some early Christians chose to live in poverty in desert caves in order to find their way to worship God apart from the noise and corruption of the city. Others joined monastic communities in order to separate from society while strengthening each other. Paul traveled from city to city, teaching his truth and attempting to build communities of faith. He wrote to those communities to respond to their questions, to advise, and to admonish them for their shortcomings. In his letter to Philemon, Paul urges his "dear friend and co-worker" (Philemon 1) to receive Onesimus, his absent slave, back into his household. Readers are not told why Onesimus left. Was Onesimus abused by Philemon?

Paul does not blame Philemon for any wrongdoing; on the contrary, he implies that Onesimus might be at fault: "If he has wronged you in any way, or owes you anything, charge that my account" (Philemon 18). Paul assumed the role of patron to Onesimus, reconciling master and slave. Could Paul have done more for Onesimus? If he really saw Onesimus as a "beloved brother" (Philemon 16), why not insist that Philemon free Onesimus?

Why didn't Paul purchase Onesimus's freedom? Still, Paul saw Onesimus as a full person, "no longer as a slave but more than a slave…both in the flesh and in the Lord" (Philemon 16), and he hopes for reconciliation and communion between Philemon and Onesimus.

Invitation

May God open our eyes to recognize structural societal sins, strengthen us to change to those structures, and when we fall short, move us to acts of kindness.

Marcie Lenk

DAY 32

As incorruptibility looked down into the region of the
waters, her image appeared in the waters, and the
authorities of the darkness became enamored of her. But
they could not lay hold of that image which had appeared
to them in the waters, because of their weakness.
Hypostasis of the Archons, "Samael's Sin" ¶5

Meditation

This text may not be on your bookshelf...yet. But if you
felt an eerie sense of recognition while reading Timothy
Snyder's *On Tyranny* (2017), *Hypostasis of the Archons* offers
a gnostic perspective on tyranny you'll want to explore.
The text acts as a valuable lens with which to view those
who claim authority in an attempt to dominate others. This
story is a response to those inquiring "about the reality of
the authorities" (*Hypostasis*, "Samael" ¶1). Readers meet the
blind chief, Samael, who declares in "his ignorance and his
arrogance" that he is the only god (*Hypostasis*, "Samael" ¶2).
He does not see incorruptibility, the divine, that dwells
above him. The archons, the "authorities of the darkness,"
that appear in this text are made in Samael's image. Their
power stems from arrogance and ignorance just as Samael's
does. They are blind to their limitations. They attempt to
exert their authority through possession and domination.
The authorities cannot comprehend that the
incorruptibility is beyond them.

Also known as *The Reality of the Rulers*, *Hypostasis* demonstrates that the reality of these rulers is one of dominance, stemming from their arrogance and ignorance. Still today we inquire about the reality of rulers. Authorities who exercise their power aggressively, who attempt to manipulate and control, must be questioned. In their blindness, they cannot comprehend their accountability for their actions. However, when these authorities seek to possess, they cannot—they are weak. Our spirit runs like water through their tightly grasping fingers.

Invitation

Who or what attempts to claim authority over you? How do you resist it? How do you allow it?

Kerri Miller Gibbs

DAY 33

The rulers took counsel with one another and said,
"Come, let us cause a deep sleep to fall on Adam." And
he slept. Now, the deep sleep that they caused to fall on
him, and he slept, is ignorance.

Hypostasis of the Archons, "The Creation" ¶9

Meditation

In this section of *Hypostasis of the Archons* we find an
alternate version to the Genesis story which describes the
creation of Adam and Eve. In *Hypostasis*, the *rulers* create
the first human. They imbue him with a soul, but cannot
animate him (*Hypostasis*, "The Creation" ¶4). Only when
incorruptibility/spirit descends upon the body does he
become fully alive and receive the name Adam (*Hypostasis*,
"The Creation" ¶5).

In today's reading, I keep coming back to Adam's sleep
being named ignorance. The rulers, in *their* ignorance, their
arrogance, cannot fully create a living human being. Then,
after the divine spirit animates Adam, the rulers seek to
regain control over their creation by moving him into a
state of ignorance. To be ignorant means that we lack
knowledge, education, or comprehension. We are
unaware—intentionally or unintentionally. The rulers
intentionally move Adam into this state to benefit their
own agenda. Their act separates Adam from the Divine,
casting him into the rulers' own image rather than that of
the Divine.

I wonder about Adam's sleep—did he know what was being taken from him? Did it feel like a dream? Or a nightmare? The rulers yet again demonstrate their arrogance, their quest for power, in the deliberate manipulation of another. Perhaps they felt entitled because they viewed Adam as their creation, not as a person in his own right. But in reality, the rulers' actions only underscore their own ignorance.

Invitation

How is ignorance at work in your life? Intentionally? Unintentionally? What can help you begin the shift from asleep to awake?

Kerri Miller Gibbs

DAY 34

Then the one who had received the one talent also came forward, saying, "Master, I knew that you were a harsh man, reaping where you did not sow, and gathering where you did not scatter seed; so I was afraid, and I went and hid your talent in the ground. Here you have what is yours." But his master replied, "You wicked and lazy slave! You knew, did you, that I reap where I did not sow, and gather where I did not scatter?"

Matthew 25:24–26

Meditation

The parable of the talents (Matthew 25:14–30) offers an example of Jesus's teachings about the kingdom of heaven. Here, Jesus tells the story of a man going on a journey who calls three of his slaves and entrusts his money with them. Two of them invest what has been given to them in order to receive more and to gain further trust of their master. The third, however, buries their portion, because they understand their master to be a harsh man. At some level in this parable, those who are enslaved are awarded an amount of trust. First, they are left with their master's money and, as such, are able to serve as his proxy. Second, there is a certain level of knowledge or education that is attributed to each of the three enslaved persons. The first two have the knowledge to go forth and make additional profit for their master. The third has the knowledge of the immoral things that their master is doing and the capability to speak against these wrong-doings. After standing up to their master, the slave is stripped of all their belongings, assumed worthless, and thrown away into the darkness.

Often, standing up for morality against the wrongdoings of the world can end in this isolation. During this season of Lent, may we allow ourselves to understand that Jesus, too, experienced this isolation in his work of advocating against the wrongdoing of others.

Invitation
As we journey through times of feeling isolated for standing against the wrong, may we find comfort in knowing these moments were experienced by the one who provided us the example of perfect morality.

Emily Davis

PALM SUNDAY

For I am the first and the last.
I am the honored one and the scorned one.
I am the whore and the holy one.
I am the wife and the virgin...
I am she whose wedding is great,
and I have not taken a husband.
I am the midwife and she who does not bear.
I am the solace of my labor pains...
I am the slave of him who prepared me.
I am the ruler...
I am the silence that is incomprehensible
and the idea whose remembrance is frequent.
I am the voice whose sound is manifold
and the word whose appearance is multiple.
I am the utterance of my name...
Give heed to me.
Thunder, Perfect Mind

Meditation

Through the ministry of Jesus we know that God wants to be found. God wants the whole cosmos to enjoy her salvation, but we often look for the Divine and her salvific work in places too expected. Many figure God as a white man with power to do anything, lightning ready to flash from his fingers, which is one understanding of divinity. Like lightning, however, ideas about God are incomplete without the rolling resonance of thunder.

Thunder, Perfect Mind is an ancient sacred poem in which the Divine discloses herself by bending all the categories of the social, political, and philosophical world. She is the *this* and the *that*, the barren and the many-times parent, the slave and the master, the wife and the mother of the same person, etc. Seemingly opposite, absurd, or unnatural pairings exist within her. Conventions that preference the male, the free, or the dominant are frustrated because the divine embodies women, slaves, children, and the aging— an extremely equalizing measure for antiquity. And yet, even as *Thunder* dwells in and with the oppressed of its day, the Divine is paradoxically found in the powerful, too. Her identity shifts and shadows just as hearers think they have even the slightest whisper of an idea of who she may be.

Through this cacophony *Thunder* resounds with the divine invitation to know God in, around, through, and beyond our constructs and understandings. Even as she confounds our expectations, her thunder calls and encompasses the whole of life.

Invitation

How might God confound your expectations? How might you listen for the all-encompassing and all-surprising thunder of God's character today?

Leanna Coyle-Carr

DAY 35

As in all the churches of the saints, women should be silent in the churches. For they are not permitted to speak, but should be subordinate, as the law also says. If there is anything they desire to know, let them ask their husbands at home. For it is shameful for a woman to speak in church. *1 Corinthians 14:33b–35*

Meditation

Can you imagine all the victims of sexual assault; victims of domestic and verbal abuse, or better yet ignored; innocent victims who sit in the shadows of shame in church as they suffer in silence?

The church should not be a space of oppression. This is not the purpose of the church.

During this season of Lent, the church should repent to women for its complicity in suffering and shame by way of silence. Globally, women have helplessly grieved, suffering with no voice. Shouldn't the church be a place that gives voice to their pain?

Jesus came to empower the broken and give voice to the voiceless. The church must be that space for the broken and voiceless.

Women must arise out of the shadows of silence that have subjugated them for years.

Invitation

Jesus sits in solidarity with the broken and voiceless. We pray with each woman that is suffering in silence and is afraid to voice her pain.

During this time of self-examination and reflection, we pray that the Holy Spirit will reveal your pain, too. In Christ's name, amen.

Mia Hash Sloan

DAY 36

Soon afterwards he went on through cities and villages,
proclaiming and bringing the good news of the kingdom
of God. The twelve were with him, as well as some
women who had been cured of evil spirits and infirmities:
Mary, called Magdalene, from whom seven demons had
gone out, and Joanna, the wife of Herod's steward Chuza,
and Susanna, and many others, who provided for
them out of their resources.

Luke 8:1–3

Meditation

Growing up, there were things women just didn't do.
Women didn't spit on the baseball diamond. Women
didn't lead, and if they did, it was with a male's approval.
Women were subjected to their own demons for being the
"lesser sex," much like this text implies. At first glance, it
appears that the text is trying to illustrate women's inability
to function without some sort of influence in her life,
demonic or otherwise. Yet perhaps the text illustrates an
important and functional role for women in ancient
culture. It is quite easy to see how women have been
maltreated and abandoned throughout time. This is true,
and there is no excuse for the way women have been
treated. However, is important not to read patriarchal male
influence into the text. This is particularly true today.
Although the reality is that women, men, and non-binary
folks remain unequal, there has been incredible and

insightful work done to create equality in every age. This is a hopeful reminder of God's true plan and purpose for us as the beloved ones. This truth is encouraging when, some days, you certainly don't want to get out of bed and deal with the world. Still, you are living. You are breathing. You matter.

Invitation
In times of temptation to see gendered oppression as limiting, recognize the women who have been influential in your own life to get you to where you are now. Meditate on their faces and validate their existence. We are all the beloved.

Gretchen Joy Gabrielson

DAY 37

Let the same mind be in you that was in Christ Jesus,
who, though he was in the form of God,
did not regard equality with God
as something to be exploited,
but emptied himself,
taking the form of a slave,
being born in human likeness.
And being found in human form,
he humbled himself
and became obedient to the point of death—
even death on a cross.
Philippians 2:5–8

Meditation

In the passage for today we are reminded that God took
on the form of a human and submitted God's self to the
consequences of a human existence: vulnerability,
exploitation, and death. Instead of exploiting the power
that comes with being God, Christ comes to us in the form
of the lowest of society—a slave. While we expect him to
come in power, he comes as one of the powerless.

Then he speaks out. He challenges the systems of
power. He overturns tables. And society treats him as they
treat those who threaten their power. Christ is killed
because slaves are not allowed to challenge the empire.

Seeing Christ as a slave is often uncomfortable. This
text was read in the southern United States to slaves to

support their condition being tied to Christ; however, this text is not meant to be justification for slavery. Though we like to find ourselves in the radical love and hospitality of Christ, it is more likely we find ourselves in the empire.

We fail to listen to the full-time employee that cannot feed her family on her minimum wage salary or the peoples who find themselves displaced in the name of corporate profit. We fail to listen to the voice of Christ.

What if we listened to those losing their healthcare? What if we listened to those finding themselves in poverty? Maybe then we'd find the voice of Christ.

Invitation

God of the disenfranchised, help me listen more closely for the voices of those we have pushed aside and to see Christ in their struggles. Amen.

Sarah Parker

MAUNDY THURSDAY

Blessed are those slaves whom the master finds alert when he comes; truly I tell you, he will fasten his belt and have them sit down to eat, and he will come and serve them. *Luke 12:37*

Meditation

Doesn't everyone deserve a seat at the table? When looking into this text we see that enslaved persons are not welcomed at the table when they have not been obedient. Yet we must remember that God has never intended for God's children to be enslaved. Therefore everyone deserves a seat at the table. We may not all do the same things, we may not handle things the same way, but we all deserve to sit at the table.

This text shows how the children of God are oppressed, because the only "slaves" that are blessed are those who are fully awake when the master comes. As stated before, we were never meant to be slaves to anything and certainly not slaves to people.

It is important that we find that God has prepared a meal for all people and that we should all be able to sit at the table and eat. Please understand that you don't have to be fearful that the "Master" will come to beat you with his belt. You deserve a place at the table. May pastors, church leaders, and laity understand the significance of having everyone sit at the table together. We are not slaves. We are humans who were created by God, and we all deserve the same treatment and a place at the table. Remember, fear should not be at the table, but joy, love, peace, hope, forgiveness, and so much more should. May we all sit at the table and eat from the abundance of God.

Invitation

I challenge every church to give everyone a seat at the table without being fearful of what they might say or do.

James H. Wilkes Jr.

GOOD FRIDAY

"In their clutches she became a tree and left before them her shadowy reflection resembling herself, and they defiled it foully".

Hypostasis of the Archons, Adam and Eve in the Garden¶1

Meditation

In this section of *Hypostasis*, we find those ignorant, arrogant rulers continuing their pursuit of incorruptibility (see Day 32 and Day 33). This time, they think they've got her. No longer a reflection in the water, incorruptibility lives in the human Eve. Yet when they try to lay hands on her, she again slips through their fingers, becoming a tree and leaving behind her shadowy reflection (*Hypostasis*, "Adam and Eve in the Garden" ¶1). But this text glosses over the fact that this "shadowy reflection" is the living, breathing human Eve. The authorities "foully defile" a living, breathing human—a living, breathing human called *it*. Incorruptibility saves herself by abandoning Eve to the rulers' brutality.

I continue to wrestle with this image. Admittedly, the original audience for this text had a different system for viewing and valuing body, soul, and spirit. They may well have cheered incorruptibility for a clever escape from the bumbling authorities. But for today's reader—for me as a reader—I feel a sense of abandonment by the spirit which culminates in the brutal gang rape of Eve. She didn't have the ability to turn into a tree. In her humanity, Eve could be overpowered by the "authorities." In a moment, everything changed. One minute she was living peacefully with the in-dwelling incorruptibility; the next, she was in the dirt being brutalized, defiled foully, by a gang of violent, arrogant bullies while incorruptibility fled. The Divine fled, leaving Eve alone. I wonder from which experience did Eve find it most difficult to heal. The savage violation of her body? Or the abandonment of the spirit?

Invitation

How have you been wounded? When have you felt abandoned by spirit? Think of where your healing lies. What does it look like? Who is part of your process? Where do you find respite?

Kerri Miller Gibbs

HOLY SATURDAY

When Jesus saw his mother and the disciple whom he
loved standing beside her, he said to his mother,
"Woman, here is your son." Then he said to the disciple,
"Here is your mother."

John 19:26–27

Meditation

At the cross we see what love looks like. The cross is where
we learn what it means to love with open arms. This kind
of love is not safe. It costs more than we can bear. All the
"important" people avoid this place. Neither Pilate nor
Herod are here. In fact, only two disciples—Mary
Magdalene and John—along with Mary, Jesus's mother,
made it. The rest are playing it safe, hunkered down. When
we love to the end, we are set free from our safe boxes and
our small lives. We know what matters and what doesn't.

Alan Jones once said, "Love is the hammer that nails
you to the cross."[2] Love is what has brought Jesus' mother,
his mother's sister, Mary Magdalene, and the lone male
disciple, John. And something happens. Jesus says that the
old boundaries don't matter anymore. He makes a new
community and a new way of connecting to one another.
He says to his mother, "Here is your son," and to John,

---

[2] Alan Jones, lecture at the Spiritual Formation Summit, Kanuga
Conference Center, Hendersonville, NC, April 2002.

"Here is your mother." Our old ways of mapping the world have disappeared. The boundaries have been erased. Neither gender nor station nor family ties matter anymore. What matters is your heart. What matters is your courage, which pulls you to the cross where all that separates you from the Savior is melted away. The hammer that nails us to the cross is the force that creates the Beloved Community.

Invitation

In this holy time may we remember this love: the force that can turn the world right-side up.

Porter Taylor

EASTER SUNDAY

I do not call you servants/slaves any longer, because the servant/slave does not know what the master is doing; but I have called you friends, because I have made known to you everything that I have heard from my Father. You did not choose me but I chose you. And I appointed you to go and bear fruit, fruit that will last, so that the Father will give you whatever you ask him in my name. I am giving you these commands so that you may love one another. *John 15:15–17*

Meditation

"I have called you friends," Jesus says in John 15:15, and in doing so, he announces a new way of being in community, not only with one another but also with God. Friends share plans and purposes with each other. Friends imagine and build relationships of trust and generous grace. Friends advocate for each other, even when the cost is giving one's life for the other.

"I have called you friends," Jesus says, and in doing so, Jesus turns the master-slave system on its head by making a clear and radical distinction between servanthood and friendship. The two cannot exist together. True friendship where people abide in God's love? That kind of friendship eradicates slavery.

In these few verses, Jesus crumbles hierarchies—divine and human—and "commands" those gathered around him to relate to each other as equal collaborators with God in the work of bearing fruit that lasts. And what is this fruit that lasts? Slavery dies on the vine along with other oppressive, life-denying forms of relating to each other while friendship—Jesus' radical form of friendship—endures to transform the world.

Invitation

Reading Jesus' words in today's social media milieu invites us to consider anew what it means to "friend" other people. Consider. As we "friend" people in our lives, how do we do so in such a way that we embody Jesus' call to undo slavery and give birth to communities where love flourishes?

Jill Y. Crainshaw

BIBLIOGRAPHY

All quotations from the Bible are the New Revised Standard Version unless otherwise noted.

Acts of Paul and Thecla. Translated by Jeremiah Jones. Found at:
https://www.pbs.org/wgbh/pages/frontline/shows/religion/maps/primary/thecla.html

Gospel of Mary. Found at:
http://gnosis.org/library/marygosp.htm

Letter of the Churches of Vienna and Lyons to the Churches of Asia and Phrygia. Excerpts from Eusebius, History of the Church 5.1. Found at:
https://sourcebooks.fordham.edu/source/177-lyonsmartyrs.asp

Letters to Trajan. Pliny the Younger. 10.96-97. See translation at:
https://www.pbs.org/wgbh/pages/frontline/shows/religion/maps/primary/pliny.html

Martyrdom of Perpetua and Felicitas. Translated by Herbert Musurillo. Found at:
https://www.pbs.org/wgbh/pages/frontline/shows/religion/maps/primary/perpetua.html

Reality of the Rulers (Hypostasis of the Archons). Translated by Willis Barnstone and Marvin Meyer. Found at: http://gnosis.org/naghamm/Hypostas-Barnstone.html

AUTHOR BIOGRAPHIES

Aaron Coyle-Carr currently serves as a pastoral resident at Wilshire Baptist Church in Dallas, Texas, where he also shares a backyard homestead with his wife, Leanna.

Leanna Coyle-Carr finished her M.Div. degree in December, 2017, and moved to Dallas, Texas. She writes a lot about God, creation, and embodiment while also working toward her Master Gardener certification. Blogging is the reality; revolution is the dream.

Emily Davis is a third-year M.Div. student at Wake Forest University School of Divinity. She is an ordained Baptist minister and plans to pursue congregational ministry after completing her M.Div.

Marc DeCoste is a third-year student at Wake Forest University School of Divinity. He serves as youth director at Calvary Moravian Church in Winston-Salem, NC, and currently wishes to pursue ordination in the Episcopal Church.

Taina Diaz-Reyes is originally from Tucson, AZ, but considers herself to be from many places due to her travels with her mobile military family. Growing up in the DC-metro area, she was raised in Lutheran and non-denominational churches until her junior year of high school, when she joined the youth group of a Pentecostal church in College Park, MD. She now describes herself as Luthercostal. She holds a B.A. in geography and sustainability at the George Washington University. Her interests in food and environmental justice led her to continue her education at Wake Forest University, where she is completing a dual M.Div./M.A.in divinity and sustainability. She hopes to complete a Ph.D. in sustainability, focusing on the relationship between ethnography, food justice, and climate change.

Jana Dye is a second-year student at Wake Forest University School of Divinity and a graduate of Georgetown College. She identifies with the Baptist faith tradition. After receiving her M.Div. she plans to pursue congregational or non-profit ministry opportunities.

Gretchen Joy Gabrielson grew up in Massachusetts and New Hampshire for most of her young adult life. A graduate of Furman University with a B.A. in communications studies, Gabrielson is currently a second-year M.Div. student at Wake Forest University. Her interests include college or hospital chaplaincy.

Elizabeth O'Donnell Gandolfo is Earley Assistant Professor of Catholic and Latin American Studies at Wake Forest University School of Divinity. She is a constructive theologian with current research interests in ecclesiology and practices of remembering historical suffering.

Kerri Miller Gibbs, a third-year M.Div. student, enjoys reading, writing, photography, and all things Scottish. She continues to discern what life after graduation may look like, but knows it must involve space for creativity, reflection, and family.

Latricia Giles was born and raised in the Bronx, NY. Latricia is currently a third-year M.Div. student at Wake Forest University School of Divinity and is counting down the days until graduation. When she is not studying, she enjoys catching up on reality television and playing basketball.

Marcie Lenk lives in Jerusalem, where she is Director of Christian Programming at the Shalom Hartman Institute. A Jew with a doctorate in early Christianity, she teaches Christian and Jewish texts to Jewish, Christian, and Muslim groups.

Andrea Marulanda-Gutiérrez was born in Cali, Colombia, South America. She graduated with a B.A. from Bethel University in Tennessee and is currently pursuing a M.Div. at Wake Forest University School of Divinity.

Veronice Miles is Visiting Professor of Preaching at Wesley Theological Seminary in Washington, D.C. For a decade, she was a professor of preaching and religious education at Wake Forest University School of Divinity. Attentive to the formative and transformative potential of preaching, Dr. Miles is committed to helping individuals and communities discover pathways for living the life of faith in word and deed. She is ordained Baptist and has participated in various facets of church and community ministry for more than 40 years.

Aubrey Naugle is a high school junior in Shillington, PA. After she graduates high school, she hopes to study sports medicine and lead in the community by teaching women how to love themselves and to start their journey toward leading a happy and healthy life.

Sarah Parker is in her last year of studies at Wake Forest University School of Divinity. She has a passion for the local church and congregational ministry and is seeking ordination in the Baptist tradition.

D'Najah Pendergrass is the Assistant Director for Residence Life at Wake Forest University. In mentoring staff and students alike she is able live out her passion for relationships and authenticity, embodying the good news of the Gospel through love of neighbor and care for the least of these.

Erica Saunders is a student at Wake Forest University School of Divinity. She plans to pursue doctoral study of the New Testament, especially Paul's letters. She also aspires to ordination in the Baptist tradition.

Katherine A. Shaner is Assistant Professor of New Testament at Wake Forest University School of Divinity. She is also an ordained pastor in the Evangelical Lutheran Church in America. Her book, *Enslaved Leadership in Early Christianity*, was the basis for the "Women and Slaves in the New Testament" course that produced this book of meditations. In classrooms, in faith communities, and in the public square, she challenges leaders to listen for the voices of people who are usually left out of our stories in our biblical texts and in our histories of justice.

Mia Hash Sloan is a Pastoral Director at St. Peter's Church and World Outreach Center. She has an intense passion to help young ladies to discover their full Divine potential at an early age. It is through this life's work and labor of love, under the divine guidance of the Holy Spirit, that she birthed two unique movements: Girl Power and Girls on the Move. Both movements breathe liberative holistic well-being for young girls and women. Mia is a native of Wytheville, VA, and currently residing in Winston-Salem, NC. She attended Winston-Salem State University and will receive her M.Div. from Wake Forest University School of Divinity in May, 2018. She is the youngest of four children to Bishop James C. and Lady Joyce Hash, the wife of Jayson D. Sloan, and a loving mom to the best children in the world, J'lyssa, Jayson James, and Jillian Isabella.

Porter Taylor joined the Wake Forest University Divinity School in 2017 as Visiting Professor of Episcopal Studies. Previously, he was the Bishop of the Episcopal Diocese of Western North Carolina. He holds a Ph.D. from Emory University and is the author of two books: *To Dream as God Dreams* and *From Anger to Zion: An Alphabet of Faith*.

Morgan Wehrkamp is a third-year student in the M.Div. program at Wake Forest University School of Divinity, graduating in May, 2018. She received a B.S. in biology and B.A. in religion from Augustana University in Sioux Falls, SD, before coming to Wake Forest. Using both bachelor degrees in her current context, much of her academic focus has been placed Old Testament studies and engaging the field of ethics.

James H. Wilkes, Jr. serves as the Senior Pastor of Elon First Baptist Church in Elon NC. He is the son of James H. Wilkes, Sr., and the late Deborah Wright Wilkes. He is married to Melia Olivia Wilkes. Wilkes desires to show and spread the love of Christ in the world.

Angel Woodrum is a third-year M.Div. student at Wake Forest University School of Divinity. Her plans upon graduation center around care of creation through sustainable, regenerative agriculture.

G. Travis Woodfield is a third-year divinity student at Wake Forest University. His ministry interests include hospital chaplaincy, empowering laity to claim their theological voice, and working with congregations who are at the end of their life.

ACKNOWLEDGEMENTS

The writers of this book have more people to acknowledge than we could possibly name. We are especially grateful to our invited contributors who were not part of the "Women and Slaves in the New Testament" course. Erica Saunders precisely and thoroughly copy-edited the manuscript before publication. William P. Kane, Director of Digital Publishing at the Z. Smith Reynolds Library at Wake Forest University (WFU), enthusiastically walked us through the process of type-setting and production. Finally, the WFU School of Divinity agreed to make the book available to students and alumna/ae for Lent 2018. For supportive colleagues, loved-ones, and communities, we are indeed thankful.

25209148R00071

Made in the USA
Columbia, SC
03 September 2018